Diane

369 DAYS

How to Survive a Year of
Worst-Case Scenarios

D1205827

Michael Levitt

Printed in the United States of America

Published by Author Academy Elite
P.O. Box 43, Powell, OH 43035

www.AuthorAcademyElite.com

Paperback ISBN-13: 978-1-64085-055-2
Hardcover ISBN-13: 978-1-64085-056-9
E-book ISBN-13: 978-1-64085-057-6

Library of Congress Control Number: 2017909167

CONTENTS

FOREWORD

Suffering personal loss impacts us all.

Each of us will encounter losses in life, which will affect us in different ways, depending on the type of loss. How we respond to loss will determine the long-term impact on us and our families and friends.

Throughout his career and life, Michael Levitt gave of himself to help others be the best they can be. However by doing this, Michael didn't focus on himself, which led to the most difficult year in his life.

As a result, Michael's health took a negative turn, which kicked off a series of dominoes to fall. Michael Levitt navigated through these falling dominoes with a positive attitude, and a drive to get back on his feet, no matter how hard he was knocked down.

Throughout the experiences Michael describes in his book, you won't sense a victim mentality mindset, but the attitude of how to move on from these losses and become better than before.

The experiences with these losses allowed Michael to simplify his life, and create different strategies to better shape his daily life. Michael shares these tools with others, to help people avoid the pitfalls he faced, during 369 Days of his life.

Michael injects humor and touching personal stories into 369 Days, to help show that even when facing significant loss, you can still enjoy life and grow as a person. The book will show you how a positive attitude will help you come out of life's losses stronger and better than before.

June 2017   Kary Oberbrunner

INTRODUCTION

You might be thinking, "What is this book about?" Welcome! My name is Michael, but you can call me Mike, Michael, Hey You, or whatever you feel comfortable with.

This book is about redemption. It's a real life, in-the-flesh story about someone who had accomplished their life goals by age forty, and lost everything in a period of 369 days from 2009 to 2010. What do people fear losing in their lives? Typical responses are their home, or their jobs. Others will say losing their health, or losing their cars. In 369 days, I experienced every one of those losses. All those fears came true.

A year of worst-case scenarios happened to me. Devastating, to be sure, as some wounds take a very long time to heal. The key to surviving a loss, let alone many losses, is to be positive through the storms.

Those events happened seven years ago, so why write a book about it? Why now? Time has allowed me to reflect on how those 369 days laid a foundation for significant changes and career growth. I know many leaders and people of all walks of life who are not protecting themselves from burnout, and who have no boundaries to protect them from pain and struggles. The struggle is real.

I have thirty years of professional experience (plus two years working at a grocery store, which is where you learn customer service really fast). Over those three decades, I've picked up a lot of tips, tricks, and tools. I've learned so much. Thankfully I'm still learning, and my goal for this book is to share with you the experiences I've faced, and to show you how to navigate through your life and (hopefully) avoid what happened to me. That should be the goal of any advice: to help others avoid the challenges you've faced, because there are plenty of challenges in life to choose from.

The first part of this book tells my story—the mistakes I made, and what I learned along the way. The second part is a practical, six-step guide to help you avoid burnout.

Shall we begin?

CHAPTER 1

IN THE BEGINNING...

How does a kid who grew up in Pontiac, and Waterford, Michigan end up in Toronto, Ontario?

I know, I know. Toronto, *Canada?* That frozen wasteland full of beavers and igloos? How did a guy who, for the first two decades of his life, never lived more than a ten-minute drive away from his parents' place, end up in *Ta-ronnah?* (Pronounce that with a *heavy* Don Cherry accent.)

Sixteen years ago, we were still dealing with the aftermath of 9/11 (Ever notice that the Euros don't call it 11/9? Always seemed weird to me). I was working at an Internet start-up (you don't hear *that* phrase anymore) in downtown Chicago.

After many steps, multiple career changes, lots of moves (I *hate* moving), and lots of lessons learned, I ended up moving north of the border.

Now, here I am, in the land of poutine and Tim Hortons. (No, I didn't miss an apostrophe there. It *used* to be Tim Horton's, but the apostrophe cost millions of dollars in printing, so the punctuation took it in the teeth, much to the chagrin of English teachers throughout the land.)

Oh, before we go much further, let me explain the stuff (in these curved brackets). I started using the (parentheses) in my writing long ago. I'm not sure why I use 'em, but I'm guessing it has something to do with a written version of ADHD (I've always wanted one of those AD/HD shirts that look like the AC/DC band logo, but I don't want to offend people who genuinely suffer from the disorder).

Anyway, back to Pontiac, Michigan. Pontiac is named after Chief Pontiac (look him up—interesting guy), as well as the name of a "Generous Motors" (GM) line of cars, which they tragically eliminated in 2010.

The City of Pontiac is a classic example of putting all your eggs in one basket. When GM left town, so did the lifeblood of the city. Yes, people still live there, and there are pockets of viability, but it has never returned to the glory of yesteryear.

Of course, you could say that about every town. I don't think we're supposed to stay the same. We're supposed to change, try new things, explore, invent, and thrive. I'm thankful for my time and experiences in Pontiac. They shaped me, and they shaped how I deal with different cultures. Growing up in Pontiac, my school was about 75 percent African-American, 20 percent Caucasian, and 5 percent Hispanic. Thus, I was a minority in the eyes of society. I was too young to care.

I only had the sixteen-count box of Crayola crayons as a child. I eventually would be bestowed with the infamous sixty-four-count box, with that piece-of-crap "sharpener" that didn't sharpen anything—but until that day, my color vocabulary was limited to the labels on those sixteen little tubes of wax.

One time, when someone said that my friend was black, I shot back, "he's not black, he's brown, and I'm peach, not white." I didn't know much about the labels society gave different groups of people, and I didn't care. All I knew was that this guy needed to get his Crayola colors straight!

I still don't care what color you are. You're a human being, with a soul, a heart, a mind, hurts, joys, triumphs, and stories. You matter to me.

I had a great childhood, a great brother, loving parents, and friends whom I still have to this day, nearly forty years later. I knew at an early age what I would likely do: become an accountant. It might sound boring to you, but it was the most exciting subject in the world to me! I knew I would enjoy this field, because I loved reading the backs of baseball cards (the 1978 Topps Cards are still the best set of baseball cards ever). I would look at the stats and figure out how they calculated those statistics. #NerdAlert

I did well in school, and continued that way in college (there were a few semesters that were iffy, but I still passed!). My younger years were filled with adventure, and . . . well, you know what your teenage years and early adult years looked like. I am beyond thankful that social media did not exist back then. The things that happened would make Snapchat blush (I'm a good boy, Mom, honest!).

My first job out of high school, and throughout my college years, was with a CPA firm in my hometown. I spent eight years there, and the foundations that experience created continues to impact how I do things today.

In the mid-1990s, I got married, and my wife and I spent eighteen months in Florida, the Sunshine State. I was tired of the Midwest weather, and I wanted something warm and consistent. We got just that—mid-nineties temperatures for eight months straight! Winter was cooler, but still quite warm.

By fate, just when I started missing the change of seasons, I learned that the software company my employer used was hiring IT network installers in Chicago. Through my long-time buddy Mark, I was hired. I left Florida at seventy-two degrees, and arrived in Chicago to negative twenty-seven degrees—nearly a hundred-degree swing. *What have I done?* I asked myself as my teeth chattered in the subzero cold.

The next decade I was in the IT field, working for a large software firm, an executive recruitment firm, a division of the Big Three automakers, and then a large Internet market research firm. Back in the 90s, there were not enough IT personnel to go around, so switching jobs for pay increases was the norm.

Then the dot-com bubble went *pop!* and IT jobs started disappearing left and right. My wife and I had started a family, and I was looking for something a bit more stable than the IT world.

Every company needs to keep track of spending, so I returned to the bean-counting world.

I worked for a small software and consulting firm in the Detroit area for four years. As my daughters were approaching school age, and because of the current economic struggles that Michigan was facing, we decided that Michigan, once again, would not be where we should stay. We explored moving back to Chicago, but family and friends were in Detroit, so we decided to move to Windsor, Ontario, Canada, which is right across the river. My wife is from Windsor, so that would be the gateway for me to immigrate to the Great White North.

Two years and several thousand dollars later, we moved to Canada. I received my Canadian citizenship 2011, so now I can vote in two countries. (Note: I will not have any political conversation in this book. It's a no-win situation. I love everybody!)

After crossing the US-Canada border for work for three years, I finally found a job close to home in Windsor. The job market is limited in Windsor, so being an American didn't help. They would rather employ a Canadian than an American. That's understandable, but my personal perspective is different. I don't care where you're from. Can you do the job? Do you fit in our culture? You're hired!

I saw an advertisement in the local paper for an administrator for a brand-new medical clinic. I looked at the details of the job, and thought, *What the heck, I'll go for it.* It was around the corner from home, and the compensation was good.

A few weeks later the phone rang, and the organization wanted to meet me. So I interviewed with them. Then, there was a second interview, and they requested references. Thankfully, I had left most of my jobs on great terms, so I had rock-solid references from bosses, friends, and co-workers. The organization called them all. I guess they really wanted to make sure this American was all he was cracked up to be.

Apparently I was. They hired me. Eighty-five people applied for the role. They performed thirteen phone interviews, five face-to-face interviews, and three final interviews. I was the only person in the finalists who had *zero* healthcare experience. I didn't even know what the heck an Autoclave was. (Note: It's a really expensive dishwasher.) So I gave my notice, and I started my career in healthcare management.

CHAPTER 2

BUILDING A BUSINESS

Now that I was hired to run a medical clinic, the hard work was to begin. I was employee number one, which required me to do the following, all within a period of two months:

- Hire staff.
- Recruit physicians.
- Coordinate delivery of medical equipment.
- Work with contractors on construction of clinic space.
- Coordinate installation of phone system, networking, Internet, etc.

Reminder: I had *zero* medical experience. However, my start-up tool bag would come in quite handy during the first ninety days on the job.

Thankfully, I had learned that having a team of people to help with interviewing is a great idea to follow. My first hire at the medical clinic served this function, to help me interview the rest of the team. It's not the normal situation for a new hire, to be responsible to help choose your teammates, but it went great. In rapid-fire sessions, we found our nurse and our reception team.

Hire staff—check!

Next up, we had the goal of recruiting additional physicians to join the team. There were already two physicians on board, but we needed to get to four to five to be able to get additional government funding. This involved several meetings with physicians, and typically their spouses (pro tip: if your spouse doesn't like the area, don't bother moving there). These meetings involved several board members and the lead physician. Most of the meetings went well, but it was a difficult area to recruit physicians. Historically, physicians *left* that area, not the other way around. Nevertheless, we eventually added two physicians, giving us four on our team.

Recruit physicians—check!

Construction is *so* much fun (#sarcasm). It has so many built-in delays. They don't tell you this, but you can go to Vegas with bets that construction projects will run late (we'll split the winnings fifty-fifty, okay?). Our clinic site was running behind, but not too far behind schedule. The landlord was motivated to get it finished, and so was the rest of the team.

I started in August, and was supposed to work from home for the first month. One month turned into three. The reason: someone wanted our space.

The clinic was built inside of a retirement home, and a local new retiree (with enough money to move mountains, apparently) wanted the space where the clinic was being built. The clinic was about 75 percent complete when this request came in.

When we were approached about the situation, my first reaction was to say no, we're not moving. Cooler heads prevailed, though, and the move actually worked well for patients, because the clinic ended up being closer to the front of the building, and would also allow the patients to see the main area of the home, so free marketing doesn't hurt.

We had a deadline of the beginning of November to be open, as that's when the lead physician's existing lease was ending. There were zero options for extension. We were expecting to open in September. This was going to be interesting.

One small issue with the delay in opening later: medical equipment. We had ordered all the exam tables, cabinets, furnishings, computers, *everything*, with a delivery date of early September. The challenge was that, now, there was no place to put these items. So, I had to spend hours on the phone with the vendors to negotiate delays in shipment, and come up with some creative storage ideas to house a full medical clinic's worth of items until we were ready. I'm still amazed we pulled that off.

Coordinate delivery of medical equipment—finally, check!

The construction crew and architects went into sudden-death overtime. They gutted three existing retirement suites and built the clinic in six weeks' time. To this day, I'm amazed that a crew could take three apartments, gut them to the bone, and build a medical clinic—but they did!

Work with contractors on construction of clinic space—check!

I remember the Friday afternoon and evening before our first clinic day. The newly assembled team was configuring their workspaces, getting things set up and ready for usage. The beauty of this setup was that *everything* was new—computers, phones, medical equipment, exam tables, cabinetry, office furniture—*everything* was new. Talk about an ideal setup!

As I was leaving, one of the nurses was talking about a patient wanting a prescription for Levitra (an erectile dysfunction medication). I said, "My last name is Levitt, but that's close—and no I don't need to use Levitra." I cringed inwardly as soon as the words came out of my mouth. *Real professional, Mike. Way to start things off on the right foot.* I apologized for my lack of professionalism. Thankfully, the nurse wasn't offended—I even caught a hint of a grin on her face.

The first day at the clinic, the lead physician saw forty-five patients. In healthcare circles, that's referred to running on the treadmill. That's a lot of people to see in a day! We were all wiped out. The network wasn't fully installed, so we had cabling strung along to a couple rooms and to reception. Wireless Internet was working, so I could use my laptop to check emails (something, you'll find out later, that would turn out to be a huge problem).

I would periodically check with the staff to see how things were going. Other than the pseudo–network connectivity, things were working smoothly.

Coordinate installation of phone system, networking, Internet, etc.— mostly, check!

Through group effort, we brought together a great team of people. Ten years later, the physicians and the reception team are still there. I guess I'm pretty good at hiring. #HumbleBrag

The following Friday was the open house, and my foray into public speaking. All the local and provincial bigwigs were there, we had a ribbon-cutting ceremony, and there was cake. Through teamwork, we created something out of nothing. That's a pretty cool feeling.

Even though I'm an introvert (according to Myers-Briggs testing), public speaking is no problem for me. In my youth, I, like many people, was scared to speak in public. No podium was big enough to hide me! All that changed in 1990, when I came down with chicken pox.

Yes, chicken pox. At age twenty-one. I had the pox everywhere but my feet. Let that sink in for a minute. The itchiness and scabbing was unpleasant. My week consisted of applying calamine lotion and taking Benadryl. When I wasn't doing either of those things, I was sleeping or watching college basketball.

Unfortunately, I was quarantined in early March, one of the biggest times for taxes. My bosses were not pleased, and really wanted me to come in, but I explained that I was highly contagious and couldn't be around anyone.

Thanks to all the downtime, I won the office NCAA College Basketball pool that year (by a landslide). Cheating accusations abounded, but the bracket was the bracket, so they had no argument. (Thank you, UNLV Runnin' Rebels!)

I also missed a week of my college classes, including a scheduled presentation in my Business Writing class. I called the professor and let her know I was on lockdown for a week. All my professors, in fact, were quite happy with me staying home. #NoCooties

My quarantined time ended on a Saturday, so I contacted my professor and said that I was good to present my speech on Monday night. She asked if I was sure, and I verified that I was no longer contagious.

When you're twenty-one and you have chicken pox, the couple of weeks afterward can be rough on your self-image. Have you ever seen *The Fly* remake with Jeff Goldblum? There's a scene where he's all red and swollen, just prior to turning into a fly. I kind of looked like that. It was scary.

So, looking like a fly-to-be, I strolled into school. Do you have a fear of people staring at you? Well, I did, and my fear was realized at that moment. Introverts don't like to be singled out, and this one *definitely* didn't like it.

When I arrived in class, the professor pulled me aside, and said if I wanted to wait another week to present, I could. I said no, I want to present this week. So I gave my presentation. I feel bad that the class had to look at me! I guess they could've looked up at the ceiling (no cell phones back then).

After the class, several people approached me and said how brave I was for presenting when I looked as bad as I did. *Thanks . . . I think,* I thought. Looking back, this was a pivotal moment in my life. If I could get in front of an audience, looking like death warmed over, I could do it anytime. And I have.

Back to the future: over the next two years at the medical clinic, I presented what we were going to do for the community. I was in my happy place, reaching out to community members, getting connected to city leaders, meeting with high-ranking government officials. Life was good . . . or so I thought.

CHAPTER 3

BURNING CANDLE AT
THREE ENDS

I had been in my role for a little over a year, but it felt more like ten years, based on how I was feeling. Of course, there were growing pains and funding challenges that come with the territory of any not-for-profit organization. I touch on this subject (and a few more) in my e-book *Avoid Chaos! An Executive Director's Guide to Running Not-For-Profit Organizations.* #ShamelessPlug

The board of directors, being community-minded, wanted more (and more) out of the clinic, which meant at-least-weekly check-ins, numerous emails, and a lot of "guidance" along the way. In order to (try to) keep up with these demands, I was constantly checking my email. From the time I woke up (around 6:00 a.m.) until I went to bed (10:30 or 11:00 p.m.), I was constantly reading and responding to emails. Looking back, I would say 100 percent of those emails could have waited until the next day or the next week, or didn't need a reply at all.

The organization had successfully added a couple physicians to the group, which was a big deal for that area. Windsor isn't on the top of lists for physicians to relocate to. The population of just over 200,000 proves that theory. The fact that the US border was so close didn't matter when on the other side of the border was Detroit. Detroit is rebounding, and infrastructure investments are happening, but it will take a long time for it to be a complete city that's booming again. Still a lot of poverty-stricken areas there, and most physicians are not keen on living in those areas.

I had phone calls, emails, and meetings with the government on a variety of issues and topics. It all seems like busy work now, reflecting on it ten years later. The best quote I've heard a board member say or ask is, "Who are we?" Too often we would encounter overzealous community members (or physicians) who wanted to change the world, and wanted their organization to do it all. Those who try doing everything, though, will accomplish nothing. I wish more organizations would understand this. Find your niche. What are you really good at doing? Do more of that. If there are other organizations that offer what you want to offer, partner up! Government (from whom you want funding) loves partnerships like that. It costs the system less, and expands the offerings to a larger population base.

Our organization was in the midst of obtaining government funding for our permanent clinic site. We were operating at a temporary site (and by "temporary" I mean we'd been there six years). Things were getting, shall we say, "cozy." The architects forgot my office after several revisions, so it was put together at the last minute. The office was forty-eight square feet. (Do me a favor and tape off forty-eight square feet in a large room. It's not much space.) I had a desk, a chair, a guest chair, and a bookshelf in that room. It was so cramped that guests would have to stand up before I could close the door. Hey, it was good exercise!

I would joke that I wanted to be promoted to a janitorial position, because the government's space guidelines indicated that Janitor closets be fifty square feet. Good thing I was a minimalist.

The funding discussions went nowhere fast, because the government was in the midst of rolling out other clinics, and were changing the rules on how new space was to be funded.

First, it was through capital project funding. Then, it was to be paid through leasehold improvements baked into leases. Over the years, the rules have continued to flip back and forth like a fish in a boat.

I recall that in the fall of 2008, the board noticed that I was on a fast approach to burnout. I was burning the candle at three ends, which, as you will discover later on, created some issues. The board ordered me to take a week off, not to check email, and to relax. (Pro tip: it takes more than a week to unwind, especially if you've been used to eighteen-hour days for over a year.) Nonetheless, I was happy with their suggestion, and I took a week off from checking emails and from work.

The only thing I recall about that week was going into the library to read a book. I didn't have a book in mind, but I was going to read something. I don't remember what book I grabbed, but I do know that I couldn't focus or relax to read the book. Reading had been a passion of mine when I was younger, but now I couldn't do it. This should have set off several alarms for me, but it didn't. I ended up grabbing a magazine and rifling through it like I was on a lunch break.

When I returned to work, I might have been a little rested, but I was nowhere near to where I needed to be. Over the following months, the consistent emails, meetings, space planning, physician recruitment, working with contractors for expansion of existing space, and other demands of my job continued. I had the pedal pressed to the floor, and I showed no signs of letting up.

I noticed that the staff was feeling the stress as well. We had just had our second annual holiday party. Typically, in positive, healthy organizations, people have a bit of a buzz (induced by joy, not by alcohol) for some time after the party. That didn't happen after our party. Within a couple of days, people were on edge again. As a leader, it's important to discover this early, and to take steps to address the issues head on. With the workload I was taking on, I didn't do what was needed to improve the morale (at least, not at first). Working in tight quarters gets to people, so I had blamed the small clinic space for the tension, and not the personality dynamics that existed, and the pressures of new demands on the clinic.

The clinic was growing, patients were getting access to care, but the workload would not be sustainable for the team unless things changed.

CHAPTER 4

THE CARDIAC DOMINO EFFECT

I had chest pains starting May 16th, 2009. I first noticed them when I was mowing my front lawn. The lawn mower I was using wasn't heavy, but it steered like a box, so there was frequent lifting and twisting required in order to make turns. That mower was not likely to be successful on the NASCAR circuit. I thought, at first, that I had I pulled a chest muscle, because it only bothered me when I was lifting the mower.

Throughout the week, the pain would return whenever I lifted something heavy, or strained myself reaching for something. It wasn't a strong pain, but it was definitely noticeable. The pain would linger for a minute or so, then go away. This went on throughout the week. I would take pain medicine to help with the discomfort, and didn't think much else about it.

The night of May 21st, I had a very large dinner. A local restaurant had a deal that provided a disgustingly large amount of food at a very cheap price. I ate most of what was on my plate, which probably equated to three meals at once.

Later that night, as I was lying in bed, the most painful chest pain I had ever experienced forced me to sit up and clutch my chest. The pain was so severe that I was sweating. At that moment, I thought I was just experiencing extreme gas, so I went into the bathroom and tossed down a couple antacid tablets. The discomfort continued, but I was able to go to sleep.

On Friday morning, I went into work, and the pain was still there, but it was persistent instead of only aching when I lifted something. I decided to ask the lead physician at the clinic about my pain. He listened to my heart, and said that just to be safe, he would have the nurse run an echocardiogram on me.

So there I was, the boss at this clinic, taking off my clothes in front of my co-workers. (I don't recommend that you do this, unless you want to have your pals in H.R. meeting with you.)

I got hooked up with the cords and patches (called electrodes), and the nurse moved a probe around my chest. (Echocardiograms use sound waves to listen to how your blood is flowing. They also create printouts of how your blood is flowing. This test takes a few minutes.) The nurse looked at the reports, and had a perplexed look on her face. She told me she was going to show the physician, and I should just sit right here.

After the physician reviewed the report, he said they were going to run the test again. He verified that all the electrodes were connected properly, and they ran it again. Same results. They decided to send over the test results to one of the cardiologists at Hotel Dieu Grace Hospital in Windsor. I got dressed and went back to my office to check emails, and got back to work.

A few minutes later, the physician came into my office and said that the cardiologist wanted me to go to the hospital. Specifically, that the cardiologist had said, "Tell Michael to get his ass to the hospital *right now*. And tell him he can't drive."

He didn't have to tell me twice.

Reflecting on that moment, I had known something was not right with me. My dad had a heart attack at age thirty-seven. When I was told to go to the hospital, I started to recall what he had said his symptoms were during his cardiac event.

I called my wife, asking her to pick me up and take me to the hospital. I'm sure that wasn't a pleasant phone call for her to receive. She picked me up, but we stopped by the house first. (Sure, the cardiologist had said to go straight to the hospital, but I'm bad at following doctor's orders.) I packed a change of clothes and grabbed a couple of things, because I knew what spending time in the emergency room is like. It's long. It's boring. It turned out that my stay at the hospital was going to be much longer than three or four hours.

The first stop after registration was triage, and another echocardiogram. After that test, with the same results as before, I moved to a bed in "Emerg" (short for emergency room) to wait. That was around 2:00 p.m. An ER doc came by, and said that he was going to spray some nitroglycerin under my tongue. If you've never had nitro before, especially in spray format, let me fill you in on what it does:

INSTANT HEADACHE!

I'm not kidding. You get a piercing headache immediately after taking nitro. It opens up your blood vessels to improve blood flow. That's why you experience the headache, because it basically stretches all the blood vessels in your body, so your brain has a "Whoa, Nellie!" moment. The adult human body has close to 100,000 miles of blood vessels (arteries, veins, and capillaries), so you can imagine how powerful nitro is to your body.

I was also hooked up to an IV with Heparin, a blood thinner, to help prevent clotting. For some reason, Heparin made me very relaxed. It's ironic, when you think of it. There I was, lying in an ER bed, hooked up to an IV, and finding out that I'm going to be admitted to the cardiac unit as soon as a bed becomes available. My hunch is that many people would be freaking out about this situation, but I was cool as a cucumber.

I was in that ER bed for almost eight hours. I wasn't able to get up and go to the bathroom, so I had to relieve myself into a container. I *really* had to go, because I filled one whole bottle and part of a second one. The nurse was amazed that my bladder held that much (so was I).

Finally, just after 10:00 p.m., I was moved to the cardiac unit. I would call that room home for the next week. After getting hooked up and set in the bed, I sent my wife home, because I wanted her with our daughters, and for her to get some rest. I'm guessing that resting was not something she did much—if I had been in her place, I would likely have been a stress case.

On Saturday morning, around 5:15 a.m., the lights in the room were turned on, and I heard a good morning. I prefer the annoying *Beep! Beep! Beep! Beep!* of an alarm clock over that kind of wake-up, but the sentiment was nice. The cardiologist who had reviewed my echo results from Friday greeted me. We exchanged pleasantries (even though I had been sleeping and wasn't overly happy being woken up that way), and he said that the hospital would be performing an angiogram on Monday, because they didn't have a cardiologist who could perform them on weekends. *There goes my weekend!* I thought.

My hospital room didn't have cable TV, but they did wheel a TV in so I could watch videos. Meh, I wasn't interested in doing that. I had a few books that I had wanted to read, so I had my family bring them when they came to visit me in the afternoon. The Heparin was working nicely, as I was still calm and relaxed. I was in full acceptance of what was going on, without putting projecting any emotions onto what was transpiring. I was as calm as one could be.

My wife and daughters came in. Sarah, my oldest, had a hesitant look on her face when she looked at me. (She had just turned 10, so she was a bit more aware of the world than her sisters). She didn't look scared, just uncertain. Rachel, age seven, was her typical bounce-around-and-look-at-everything self, and Abigail, age six, was clinging to her mom (so my hunch is that she was a bit frightened by the situation). We had a nice visit, but I knew the girls would get bored quickly, especially without a cable TV hook-up in the room. So I let them know that it was okay to leave, and that I would see them again soon.

The rest of Saturday and Sunday are a blur, other than seeing my mom, who flew up from Florida and came to visit me on Sunday. As a parent, the last thing you ever want to see is your child lying in a hospital bed. Mom's as strong as they get, but I knew this was tearing her up emotionally. I still remained calm. I also remember hearing a ton of car horns honking on Sunday afternoon, because the Ontario Hockey League's Windsor Spitfires had won the Memorial Cup, which was being played a few buildings over from the hospital. I smiled as I lay in the bed. Windsor has had its share of hard times, so winning a hockey title was a big deal to the city.

Monday arrived—the big day! Or not. Apparently, there was a backup of patients who needed angiograms, so my condition, based on how well I did over the weekend, made it easy for them to bump me to Tuesday. While I was frustrated, I knew that there had to be patients who needed more urgent attention. I was treated very well, the delay aside. It probably helped that I was forty instead of seventy or eighty, so the people taking care of me identified with me more. The food wasn't great, but they couldn't do anything about that. Imagine no flavor (*flavour* for my Canadian brethren) in your food. That's what I was subjected to for a week—sodium-free everything. Yuck. Like I said, though, it couldn't be helped. I didn't need a lot of care while I was there, so I think that made my stay even more pleasant for the healthcare professionals in that ward.

Tuesday arrived. Angiogram day was finally here. It was my fifth day in the hospital. The angiogram procedure was done in the afternoon, and they suggested that I refrain from liquids for a while, so I got dry mouth really quick. The cardiologist cut a small incision in my right groin area, and ran a tube up to my heart. After the tube was where it needed to be, they injected a dye into my heart, to help see if there were any issues. This dye gives you a very warm sensation that travels from the top of your head, all the way down to your toes. It felt like I urinated all over the table, but I didn't at all. Mind games extraordinaire.

The cardiologist said that yep, I had two blockages. He flipped over the monitor so I could see where the blockages were. There I was, lying on an operating table, awake, looking at my heart. Surreal.

I had two blockages in the Left Anterior Descending Artery. One blockage was 60 percent, and the other blockage was 90 percent of the artery.

I found out later that the Left Anterior Descending Artery, also referred to as the LAD, has a nickname amongst the cardiology world: the widow-maker. This artery is a small artery, but it is a very important one. It supplies blood to the largest parts of the heart, and failure of this artery can cause severe heart attacks and sudden death. *Well, then*, I thought, after learning this.

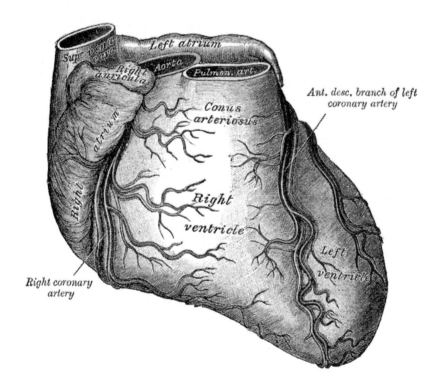

Henry Vandyke Carter - Henry Gray (1918) *Anatomy of the Human Body*

(Since I am writing this, I am obviously not dead. This is helpful to remember as I encounter the small challenges that we all face in our day-to-day lives.)

Now, the bad news: the cardiologist who performed the angiogram wasn't licensed to perform an angioplasty, which is a procedure to put stents (which look like a spring from a pen) into the blocked artery. Thus, they had to schedule another cardiologist to perform the angioplasty. (Welcome to healthcare in Ontario!)

So, I was moved out of the operating room into a recovery area. There was a problem. I was bleeding from the surgical area—quite a bit. Normally, the nurse or other healthcare professional could put pressure on the wound area, and it would clot up enough to seal up. Again, I was calm during this situation, as was the nurse, but I could tell that she was concerned. They ended up hooking up a vise to me, to press down on the wound (no joke!). I was clamped to the recovery table, like you would clamp a piece of wood you're about to saw. To this day, when I see a clamp, I think of this moment. I must admit, it was neat to see the blood shoot up from the wound just before they put the clamp on me. I'm guessing that "neat" wasn't the word anyone else in the room would use to describe the experience.

I was moved back to my room, and the clamp was left on my leg for several hours. *Don't worry; I'm not going anywhere*, I thought. (One thing I learned is that you notice back pain more when you can't move.) You might ask why they didn't sew me back up. They did, but they needed to leave an opening so the next cardiologist could operate on me and install the stents.

Wednesday was angioplasty day. On day six at the hospital, they were going to operate on me in the afternoon. I went into the same operating room as the day before and met the cardiologist. My mom and wife were there, so he greeted us all, and asked if I'd been updated on the results from the angioplasty. I said no, not other than the two blockages. He then said words that are very difficult to hear: "You've had a heart attack. You're very fortunate to be here."

Well, then.

I nodded. My mom and wife were holding back tears, trying to be strong for me. The cardiologist said he was planning to put two or three stents into my LAD (the widow-maker artery, if you were paying attention to my science lesson earlier), but that he wouldn't know for sure until he got inside my heart.

Next, I was wheeled into the procedure room, and I hopped up on the table. I felt the tube going into my groin area and up towards my heart. The cardiologist said it might pinch a little. By "pinch," I think he meant it would feel like someone dropped a car on my chest. What caused the pain was the balloon used to stretch my artery enough for the insertion of the stent. Then stent number two was installed, and he said two stents should do.

Then, it was done. I was sewn up, and shortly afterwards I was wheeled up to my room. The nurse in the cardio unit said I would likely be discharged the next day, which I was. Between then and discharge, I briefly met with a social worker to see how I was doing emotionally (still happy on Heparin!). I also met with a dietitian, who told me all the nasty food I should eat, and all the yummy food I shouldn't eat.

I remember sitting in the pick-up area, waiting for my wife to pick me up that Thursday morning. It was nice to get out of the hospital after seven days. I was their unofficial greeter for a few minutes. I said hello to everyone who was coming into or leaving the hospital! I was happy to be alive and going home, with little idea of what was to transpire over the next year.

CHAPTER 5

THE THREE RS: RECOVERY, READING, RELAXATION

One of the perks of a post-cardiac event is some downtime. I'd had my heart attack at the end of May, and my expected recovery time was three months (in the end, it was seventeen weeks). Thankfully, through the benefits program provided by my employer, we had Short Term Liability insurance. Not many organizations offer this type of coverage now, because it's pricey, but we had it as part of our benefits package.

This allowed me to recover at home, and most of my recovery took place over the summer months. I know many working adults dream of taking summers off, like they did when they were in school. It was good for me to have this time to recover, as my body had been through a little bit of trauma. #understatement

It was a significant struggle in the beginning. The first couple of weeks, I would wake up around my normal time (6:30 or 7:00 a.m.), but by 2:00 p.m., I couldn't stay awake and had to take a nap. Historically, the only time I had ever taken naps was when I was sick with a cold or flu, or on Saturday afternoons in the fall, while watching college football.

The recliner that I would sit in during my pre–cardiac event naps had been in my family for twenty years. It was a La-Z-Boy recliner, and my parents paid close to a thousand dollars for it back in 1990. We got our money's worth out of that recliner! It followed me from Michigan to Florida, from Florida to Illinois, from Illinois back to Michigan, and from Michigan to Canada. If I ever buy a recliner again, it will be the newer version of that model—best sleep ever!

The naps after the cardiac event were basically spent in bed. My energy levels were low, as my body was getting back to the new normal. Being forty years old and needing to take a nap at 2:00 p.m. is not normal. Thankfully, my energy came back, and naps are once again a weekend activity, if I take them at all. (Disclaimer: I know the health benefits of taking naps during the day, but my current position doesn't allow for that flexibility. My hope is that society will discover the benefits of midday naps, and create nap zones in places of employment!)

I went from working countless hours, every day of the week, to having nothing on my schedule but recovery, rest, and relaxation. The challenge is that I had forgotten how to relax. I had been going at full speed for so long: working long hours, following no personal boundaries, and never shutting down. I needed to re-learn how to live.

Pro tip: do not consume too much daytime television. Your IQ scores will drop dramatically. Scandals, DNA tests, TV court-rooms—none of this programming will help you grow as a person, at least brain-power wise. Your gut may grow if you spend all your time on the couch, though. Get up and move it, kids! #PublicServiceAnnouncement

A few months prior to the cardiac event, I had signed up for a book-reading program through Thomas Nelson Publishing. The program would send you books to read for free, but you had to post an honest review of the book on Amazon and other outlets. So, I started getting some books, and started reading again, after many, many years. As a child, I loved to read. My parents told me that I was able to read at age three, which from what I'm told is not normal. (But who said I was normal?)

Now that I had all the time in the world, I decided to start reading more books. I would read a book and make notes of what I learned from each chapter (which I highly recommend you do when you read any book, including this one). Of all the books I read, there's one book that stands out to me: *A Million Miles in a Thousand Years* by Donald Miller. I read Donald's book from cover to cover. I didn't stop for lunch, or anything else (other than a bathroom break). I can't recall ever doing that with a book of any length. Donald's writing sucked me into the story as if I were there, walking through the story with him. I highly recommend it.

I also spent some time volunteering at our local church. It gave me something to do during the day, so I wouldn't go stir crazy from watching DNA test results and game shows all day.

I had learned (somewhat) to relax again, to take each day as it came, and not to overly schedule it. When writing this section, I looked back at my Google calendar, and rediscovered that I was still scheduling my day. Some things never change, and it helps keep my stress at bay, because as Michael Hyatt says, what gets scheduled gets done. However, I am much better at having boundaries in my scheduling.

It was hard at first not to do any work. I had put so much time and effort into my job, it was difficult not to be involved in the day-to-day operations. How do you go from checking work emails from 7:00 a.m. until 10:00 p.m., day after day, to not checking at all? Like any addiction, it's difficult to quit cold turkey. But I did.

I was getting my energy back, and I was starting to feel better again. I knew that my life needed to go in a different direction, but little did I know how much it was about to change.

CHAPTER 6

SECOND DOMINO

While I was recovering from my cardiac event, my employer was questioning some of the decisions I had made on the job. These inquiries were about staffing moves, schedules, comp time, et cetera. I did my best to respond to these inquiries, but my answers didn't seem to appease the committee.

I sensed that things were not going to be pleasant upon my return. I had made some reporting mistakes, which were highlighted in an official letter from the organization. They also seemed upset that the benefits program I had negotiated had Short Term Liability coverage (which paid me while I was recovering from my heart attack). As I mentioned earlier, Short Term Liability insurance is pricey, but we had it.

I apologized for the reporting mistakes in a face-to-face meeting, which we had scheduled to go over items that they wanted to address. We discussed those items, I acknowledged and apologized for the mistakes as they were presented to me, and I thanked them for bringing the errors to my attention. I made them, so I owned up to them.

As summer approached its end, the organization started asking when I would be returning. The doctor gave me a note saying I could return to work on September 9th, 2009, and also a letter to give to my employer. I gave the letter to my employer, who immediately wanted to book a meeting to go over the items we had discussed before. I agreed, and met with the committee again.

After rehashing the items that were brought to my attention, the committee requested that I come up with a plan for structuring my day-to-day activities, with a detailed breakdown of each task. They gave me until the end of the week to submit my work plan.

I knew what was about to happen. (I might be dumb, but I ain't stupid.) I followed their instructions, and even used an outside consultant to help me proof read and craft a work plan that would successfully meet all of their requirements and guidelines. I submitted my response to the committee, and waited for their response.

I was called to a 3:00 p.m. meeting with the committee, which was later than we normally met (typically we met in the mornings, or just before lunch), so I knew something was up. I arrived, and my (now former) boss said that unfortunately, the organization was letting me go. He provided me a letter indicating that my work plan didn't sufficiently address their requests.
Well, then.

After that meeting, I drove to my cardiac rehab appointment. Cardiac rehab, for me, at that point, was an hour of exercising, stretching, and coaching from the medical team at the hospital. Somehow, I was able to (somewhat) purge from my mind the events from earlier in the day. It wasn't until I returned home later that afternoon that my emotions caught up with me.

After missing almost four months of work, I returned long enough for the organization to fire me. I was pissed. I sought legal counsel on the issue, and after discussing the events and situations, it boiled down to this: the employer has the right to terminate with or without cause, so the pursuit of a case in this situation would be time-consuming, costly, and potentially unsuccessful. Thankfully, my former employer and I agreed on a settlement package.

So, in 2009, my summer consisted of having a heart attack and losing my job. How was your summer?

Let's recap. May 21st I had the cardiac event. September 24th I was, to use a Jack Welch term, "de-hired" from my job. So now that I'd healed from my health concerns, my energy needed to focus 100 percent on finding a new job.

For those of you not familiar with the Windsor area of Ontario, it is a border city to Detroit. In 2009, Windsor was still impacted by the Great Recession of 2008. Remember that? When the US Government had to bail out General Motors and Chrysler, so they wouldn't go under? When the mortgage and banking industry's bad lending habits came back to bite really hard?

Windsor was (and still kind of is) tied to the automotive industry. If the auto sector is doing well, towns like Windsor and Detroit will do well, too. When the auto industry is in the toilet—well, so is the economy (and the job market) in those towns.

Looking for an upper management job in the Windsor area was very difficult. There weren't a lot of positions to begin with, and even fewer openings. Those who had those roles were pouring cement on their feet and not going anywhere, no matter how crappy the working conditions were. Detroit was worse. There was nothing available in the area. So, I had decisions to make.

I considered briefly exploring moving back to Chicago. Chicago is one of those major cities that don't really have one industry. The dot-com bomb had done some damage, but I thought there would be better opportunities there. However, my daughters were already in school, and being a patient with a chronic disease, I didn't think it would be wise to leave a country that had basic health insurance coverage, and go back to the US, where there was none. (Remember, this was 2009, so the Affordable Health Care Act was not an option.)

I started to expand my search area to the Greater Southwest region of Ontario. Specifically, I looked in London and the Kitchener-Waterloo area. Waterloo was home to Research In Motion (a.k.a. Blackberry), and there were quite a few upper management openings in that area. I sent out my MichaelLevittResume. doc to hundreds (yes, hundreds) of postings, looking to find a position.

I went on at least two dozen first interviews between July 2009 and March 2010, with at least a dozen second interviews. I interview well, because I treat the interview as a conversation, and I'm not overly nervous about the meeting. Some interviews go better than others, and the key is to be yourself, to know your role, and to be prepared for the behavioral questions, and you'll be the right fit if you match with their culture.

That's the big unknown in the interview world. The candidate doesn't really know what the culture is like at the place they're interviewing with, so it's imperative to ask probing questions about the work culture during your interviews. You should know what kinds of environments you don't like, so ask roundabout questions to see if there are any hints of that in the organization. You won't learn everything, but you'll at least get some vibes about what's going on there.

CHAPTER 7

BRIDESMAID INTERVIEWS
AND BALLOON BOY

I made several overnight trips to Kitchener-Waterloo, where I was on my own, feeling like a travelling salesperson trying to land sales. (I truly empathize with on-the-road sales people. Be kind to them. They're trying to earn a living, just like you and me.) The hotels I frequented were on the cheap end— so, a bit run down— and the beds weren't luxurious by any means. I had to do what I could to conserve money, as things were going to get tighter and tighter.

While I was sending out resumes and going on interviews, a huge world event took place that helped me feel close to my family, even though we were physically far apart. It was an event that took the US and Canada by storm. October 15th, 2009. Balloon Boy. Yes, remember Balloon Boy? The homemade balloon aircraft that was floating uncontrolled, that was (supposedly) carrying a little boy? That was must-watch TV. My wife, being a mother, was freaking out. I was glued to the coverage to the same level, as I was when the LAPD was chasing that White Bronco on the California Freeway. (Again, IQ levels drop with that type of entertainment.) People that know me will tell you that I am a sucker for police chases. Back in the late 90s, I would get pager notifications whenever there was a police chase in the US, and I bookmarked a website that would tell you where to watch online. I need help, people!

Now, back to the interviews. I had many second interviews, and even a few third interviews (talk about a vetting process!). In each case, I came in second place. Yes, second. I was the Buffalo Bills of interviewing, always losing the big game.

Part of the mindset shift that kept me motivated through this time period was that, even though the Buffalo Bills lost four straight Super Bowls, they were also four-time AFC Champions. No, they didn't win the big championship, but they were still champions. Even though I came in second way too many times, I was still a champion . . . and if I ever wanted to come in first in my interviews, I would have to maintain a winner's mindset.

Having said that, I was getting more frustrated and worried by the day. My family told me not to put too much stress on myself (I wonder why?), and that something would happen in time. That's wonderful and thoughtful advice, but when you're watching the numbers in your bank account continue their steady downward march, with no income coming in, natural fears creep in.

At this point, my heart attack was the furthest thing from my mind, other than paying for the medications I was on. Without insurance, the medications were costing over six hundred dollars per month. (That's over $7,200 per year for you math wizards.) Don't get sick, kids—it's a nasty hit to the budget. A perfect storm was a possibility: I had no money to pay bills, no money to buy medicine, and significant stress from looking for work and coming up second.

There was one job market that I had been avoiding to look for opportunities, because I had distaste for the city. Reflecting on this now, it was a very foolish mistake on my part to ignore the opportunities offered there, and that mistake made a huge impact on my career.

CHAPTER 8

TORONTO AND THE THIRD DOMINO

T hings were getting tight. My severance pay was being eaten up pretty fast (it's amazing how much money a family of five can spend). I was coming up empty on the job search, and it had gotten to the point where I needed to do something drastic.

So, for six weeks (though it felt like much longer), I took a minimum wage job with a Canadian-based IT support organization that was providing technical support for a US-based cable provider.

Yes, America, your cable TV tech support was outsourced to Canada. We even had training on how not to sound Canadian. I find this very funny, as growing up in the States I don't have a Canadian accent . . . or, at that point, I didn't *think* I did. My American family and friends say they hear a Canadian accent when I speak, and my Canadian friends claim they hear my American accent!

I was trained on how to configure the cable boxes remotely, including how to program the remotes to work with customers' televisions. It's amazing how few people know what brand of television they have when the name of the manufacturer is on the front of the TV. Years of customer service, going back to my grocery bagging days, came through again. You just have to be patient with people.

I was really good at the job and management thought I had great promise in this field. They didn't know that I had been a Director of IT and Corporate Services for a nationwide university, or had provided IT support for three international, publicly traded companies. So, yes, of course I was really good at the job! I knew more than my boss's boss knew. I wasn't going to speak up, though, as I hoped my stay here would be short.

And it was. After coming up dry on my job search in the Kitchener-Waterloo region, I reluctantly started looking for opportunities in Toronto. Yes, that dreaded city. I had fallen victim to the anti-Toronto sentiment that exists in parts of Canada. The city has a reputation of being the center of the universe (or, as Canadians would spell it, centre). At least, that's how some native Torontonians act, feel, speak, and breathe. Plus, whenever governments give money for projects, Toronto gets a big chunk.

The reason why is that, of the thirty-five million people who live in Canada, over seven million live in the Greater Toronto Area (GTA). That's 20 percent of the total country's population, all within a very small footprint. Hence the traffic on Highway 401, which fights with Los Angeles for having the worst traffic in North America.

Toronto has pretty much every culture known to planet Earth. This is a good thing—if we can get along with each other, then there's hope for humanity! The variety of food you can find in the city is staggering, especially for a guy who grew up eating typical family restaurant fare.

I had worked in a large city before (Chicago), and I wasn't overly excited about the prospects of doing it again. However, since I kind of needed a job (#understatement), I gritted my teeth and sent MichaelLevittResume.doc off to businesses in Toronto to see what would stick.

Within a couple weeks, I had three interviews lined up. I thought that seemed promising. I also had an interview in the

Guelph area of Ontario for a healthcare leadership position. (I now mentor the person who is in that role. The world is an entertaining place.)

I went on an interview in the east end of Toronto, with a large healthcare organization that also provided social services to the community. This was right up my alley. I still wasn't happy about the location, but I interviewed well.

I found out I had gotten the job on St. Patrick's Day 2010. As if I needed a reason to celebrate the holiday in the first place, now I had another!I was going to start in a couple weeks, so I had to scramble to find a place to live, and fast.

I was close to getting an offer from the place near Guelph, but I sent them a note indicating that I'd taken a position in Toronto (likely one of the best career moves I've made). My family came up on the following weekend to look at places, after finding places to rent online. (Yes kids, Internet existed in 2009.) We couldn't find any places within our budget that would fit all of us. We decided that I would rent a room, and my wife and daughters would stay in Windsor until we found a place for a family of five.

I found a room to rent in a townhouse, located in the north side of the city, which would be about twenty-five minutes west from my new job. I rented from a partially blind woman (probably why she would rent to me—she didn't have to look at me!) who was very particular and protective of her space.

Being a minimalist (before it was even cool!), I made sure that I didn't leave anything around the house, and I kept to myself in the bedroom. I went back to Windsor on weekends, so I was only at the townhouse Sunday night through Friday morning. Over time, my landlady warmed up a little, and she would cook me some dinners that were—well, unique. She had some significant vision issues, as I said, so the presentation wasn't restaurant-perfect. It was decent food, though, and I always cleaned my plate. I lived there six weeks, and I appreciated her hospitality as I continued to ease into the new job and look for a home for the rest of the crew.

I was a pretty good tenant, except for one time: I returned home from a late night dinner one night, and backed into my parking spot in the garage. I parked closer to the wall than normal, but I opened the back hatch of the minivan without any issues. What I didn't realize was that there was a fire alarm on the wall. When I closed the hatch, it grabbed the lever—and that's how you get to meet the fire department, kids!

For six weeks, I commuted from the north side of Toronto to the east side. Because my roomie was pretty independent, I spent most evenings solo, eating out, reading some books, researching places to live, and driving around Toronto to figure out where things were. My previous experiences with Toronto were strictly in the downtown area, so the suburbs were completely foreign to me.

A little after 4:00 p.m. one afternoon, I had a meeting with the Director of Community Services at my new job. Just as we were starting our conversation, my cell phone rang. The caller display said *Home*. There are a few contacts that I'll answer the phone for, no matter what. *Home* is one of them.

I answered the phone, and it was my oldest daughter. She was crying so much that I couldn't understand her. I kept telling her, "Sarah, Sarah! I can't understand what you're saying!" After about thirty seconds of this, I asked to speak to her mother. My wife came on the line and, after controlling herself, said, "They took the truck." So *that's* what Sarah was trying to say.

I responded, "What? Who's 'they'?" She replied, "I guess the bank. They've taken the truck away. We don't have it anymore." She proceeded to tell me that the person repossessing the vehicle allowed her to empty it of our personal contents, but then towed it away.

I was a four-hour drive away, and was not there to comfort my family in this traumatic experience. It must have been a very rough thing to see our truck towed away. They had to have felt powerless—I know I did. I hung up the phone, composed myself, and continued my meeting, trying to compartmentalize what had just happened. Thankfully we still had the vehicle I was using, so I could get back to Windsor that weekend.

Growing up in a family that worked in the Automotive Industry, I have never been a fan of how we are hostages to our vehicles. I wish that public transit was a more viable option to all, so you wouldn't have to sink a ton of your salary into car payments or leases. #ExcuseTheRant

It all seems like a blur now, that I've been up here for seven years. So much has happened since the move up here, career-wise. My only regret would be that I should have looked to Toronto much sooner, as a place to call home.

CHAPTER 9

DOMINO FOUR

After looking all over the Greater Toronto Area for a place to rent, we found one on the east end of Toronto. It was close to Highway 401 (a major highway in Ontario that runs east and west), and it was also within walking distance of an elementary school where our daughters could attend.

We were able to move in the middle of May 2009, which was a good time because the wintery weather was finally done. The kicker was getting everything packed to move. That was a taxing situation for the family, as I was in Toronto working, and I couldn't be in Windsor during the week to help them pack.

I spent the weekends leading up to the move in Windsor, though. In addition to packing, I worked with friends to repaint some of the rooms and repair some window trim. My wife and I were hoping to sell the house, so we spent our limited funds on getting the house ready for sale. There wasn't anything wrong with it, but anyone who's sold a home knows that if your home looks shiny and new, it'll probably sell faster.

Whenever you improve your home to sell, there's a little part of you wishing you would have done it sooner, so you could enjoy the new paint, the new trim, and appliances. But, we were closing one chapter of our lives and opening a new one in Toronto.

To help pay for all the touch-ups on the old house, we started selling off some of our new appliances; including the new washer and dryer set my parents bought us. Boy, did the buyers get a bargain on those! I'm not a big fan of the high efficiency models anyway, since they tend to have more computer parts than machine. Give me an earth-hating 1950s washer and dryer set any day, thank you very much.

We sold the refrigerator and microwave, too. Basically, if it wasn't bolted down, it was sold (except the dishwasher, that would be jerk-like to rip that out). I don't recall if we sold the stove or not. It's amazing how much I *do* remember from this period of my life, even after all the adventures that have happened since those challenging days.

Weekdays working in Toronto were spent getting fully up to speed on the new job. There were several changes being rolled out with the organization, including a rebranding exercise that made me appreciate marketing people even more. My background in accounting naturally created some tension with the marketing folk: all they want to do is spend money on ideas and dreams, and we bean counters are worried about budgets.

I was slowly getting into the groove of working again. You may recall, it had been over ten months since I had actually worked. (Job-hunting all over Ontario was a lot like working a job, but the pay wasn't great—oh, that's right, there *was* no pay.) I was getting to know the management team, the people who worked in other departments, and the people who worked for me. There were over 120 people in that organization, and they all brought different skills, backgrounds, and opinions to their roles.

One of the things I noticed about working there is that there was very little time spent on celebrating a win (this is true of most places, these days). There were some great things accomplished during my time there, and we didn't really celebrate them. One such win was securing a small delivery truck for some of our projects. Historically, the organization would rent trucks to handle picking up or delivery of goods. This adds up, not to mention that rental trucks break down a lot. When one of the directors announced the funding award for the organization, it was a "good job" from the boss, and that was that. I went to the director responsible for making the award happen, and told her, "This is a huge deal—what you've done will serve this community for several years. Celebrate this!"

We get so bogged down in the mundane, day-to-day crap that we don't take time to celebrate anymore. Our superiors say, "Get this done!" and we do it. It works well. Nothing is said. Why not? A job well done should be acknowledged! It takes time to get things done right, and when they are, there should be a period to enjoy the fruits of our labor. If you have the power to ensure that achievements are celebrated your place of employment, I beg you to do so. We need more positive reinforcement in our jobs! (I digress, but I feel passionately about this!)

Now, back to moving. A household of five people tends to create a lot of things to move. In our situation, the budget was tight, so there wouldn't be an opportunity to buy new furnishings in Toronto. What we didn't sell, we moved to the new house. We hired a moving company to move everything. We just had to pack and unpack (which is still a ton of work).

The moving company called and asked the number of rooms we were moving, and how many people. However, they didn't come to the house to actually get an inventory. This was a costly oversight. Once the movers arrived on moving day, and started packing their truck, it was apparent that it wouldn't all fit. (Insert profound profanity by Mike here.)

I asked if they had another moving truck, but they had already allocated their movers to other jobs. The issue with living in a smaller community (rather than a large metropolitan area) is that movers don't have a fleet of trucks. They have three or four, at best. I frantically called around to find a rental moving truck that was available in town. I was very fortunate to have found one on a Saturday, because I didn't want to come back to Windsor the next weekend just to load up another truck. Plus, there would be no way to prioritize which boxes to take on the first trip, as the plastic totes we used were a mixture of items from each room.

(Pro tip: Become a minimalist. Now. Consume less. You'll have more freedom and space. Trust me on this one.)

I secured the rental moving truck and went back to the house to load up the remaining boxes. The truck was almost full by the time we were done. (Once again, Mike reminds you to become a minimalist.) My family drove up with the main moving truck, and I loaded what was left into the rental truck. I did forget a couple things, but I'll discuss that later on in the chapter.

After locking up the house, one of my daughters and I hopped into the rental truck, and started the four-plus–hour drive east. For those of you who have never driven a moving truck, they're very hard to drive. They bounce around a lot if it's windy, and they make you realize how narrow some streets are, especially when you encounter roadside mailboxes. (Sorry about that.) #MailboxDown

We arrived at the Toronto home around 8:30 p.m., and the movers had just finished unloading the first truck. My truck was easy to unload, since it was mostly filled with plastic totes, which I just had them drop in the garage, and not in the house. Movers charge by the hour, people—make it quick for them, and you can do the sorting later!

Unpacking took months, because when you move from a tri-level home with a full basement to a Toronto house the size of a shoebox, your stuff won't all fit. Thus, our garage was the storage room for the entire four years we lived in that house. (Minimalism, kids, it's the bomb!)

I remain thankful that my new employer assisted with our moving costs. It would have taken several trips if we had to do it with our own funds. I'm thankful to everyone who came to help us move that day. It could've been an emotional day, but we were so busy that we didn't take time to reflect on our last day in that house. I'm thankful for the friends who helped paint and install woodwork to make the house ready for sale. You barely charged us anything for your labor. Your gifts remain with me to this day.

After we sorted through things, we realized that we had left the ladder for the kids' bunk bed at the old house in Windsor. We also had an upright piano that a family friend wanted to have. We decided I would go down there the next weekend to grab those things and to coordinate with the friend to pick up the piano.

My drive down that weekend was uneventful, and I hadn't thought much about the house other than to grab the ladder and move the piano out. I was going to spend the weekend at my brother's house in Michigan, and then stop by the old house.

I arrived at the house on Monday morning (I took a long weekend—highly recommended). When I opened the screen door, I saw a huge padlock and security panel securing the door. My house had been repossessed.

I stood there on the porch, holding the screen door, staring at the gaudy padlock. This wasn't your Home Depot quality padlock. This lock was probably a several-hundred-dollars model.

The world stopped.

I started to hear the breeze blow through the newly formed leaves in the trees. The street was quiet, as it was a normal Monday workday. I stood there, listening to the breeze, feeling nothing at first. My next feeling was something you probably wouldn't expect.

Peace.

The *final domino* had fallen.

In a year's time, I had lost:

My health.

My job.

My vehicle.

My home.

There was nothing left to lose. The season of loss was over. I was at complete peace.

I gently closed the screen door, put my hand on the brick facade, and said a quick prayer in my heart: *God, bless this home. It was a blessing to my family and me. Please bless and protect the next family that moves into it.*

I walked back to the minivan, backed out of the driveway, and drove home to Toronto.

CHAPTER 10

GROWTH AND REFLECTION

Four dominoes, in the grand scheme of things, is not a lot. I have no clue how many dominos come in a box, but unless you bought them at a garage sale, my hunch is that there are more than four in there.

The four dominoes I shared with you in this book, however, were very impactful to my family, my friends, my career, and me. One of these events, alone, could bring someone to their knees, but I apparently needed to go big or go home.

After the move (with two moving trucks) to Toronto, I've grown so much professionally. I've helped organizations change their culture for the better. I've helped save divisions of an organization from closing, and now they're thriving and doing better than ever. I've hired people who are now making a positive impact on the lives of others.

I earned a certificate in advanced healthcare leadership through the Rotman School of Management, a graduate school within the University of Toronto that is highly regarded globally. That certificate was made possible by my willingness to help and serve local government agencies in creating new and improved ways to better healthcare for patients.

I am an executive, an author, a public speaker (speaking at IT, leadership coaching and healthcare conferences), and I'm an expert on healthcare and leadership, with a focus on the lean manufacturing method and on boundaries for individuals.

If you don't establish boundaries for yourself, no one else will. You might as well get the word "welcome" tattooed to your forehead, because people will walk all over you. Boundaries are crucial.

I've gone from despising Toronto to loving it, and embracing all of its quirks. All cities have them, but now they're my city's quirks.

Each cardiologist I speak with tells me that I'm very fortunate to be alive. I forget this most days, but there are days when I realize that I'm here for a reason. This book is one of those reasons.

My hope for you is that you take my experiences to heart, and that you make whatever changes you need to make to ensure that you're living the best life you can. You deserve this, as do your family, friends, colleagues, and community.

I would love to help show you how. Visit BreakfastLeadership. com and sign up for email news, tips, occasional bad dad jokes (via Twitter), coaching, and whatever else I can show you.

Be well!

APPENDIX

CREATE YOUR SUCCESSFUL MORNING

After 369 days (and several years after that), I've picked up various techniques and tricks to help me simplify my life, to help me prevent another 369 days. BreakfastLeadership.com has more resources, podcasts, and coaching tips to help you navigate life.

A great day starts with a great beginning. How many times have you crashed onto your couch or comfy chair, completely drained from your day? If it's more than once a week, it's way too much. Your workday likely was filled with interruptions, out-of-the-blue demands, firefighting, and an overall lack of control.

Why does this happen? Because you let it happen.

You let it happen because you likely don't have structure in your daily life. Too many of us put our lives on autopilot. We show up at work, and we stand by, letting things happen *to* us, instead of having the control to make things happen *through* us.

I know all about this because I was exactly that way. My workdays were too long, and I wouldn't accomplish what I needed to do. This forced me to work nights and weekends just to keep up with the demands.

This insane lifestyle took a toll on my health, and in 2009, I had a heart attack. I was in my early forties—and by all accounts, that's too early to have a cardiac event. After a week in the hospital,

I left with two stents in my left anterior descending artery and a call to change my life.

Establishing boundaries in your life (both work and personal) isn't easy, especially if people are used to interacting with you in a certain way. More on that later—let's return to creating your successful morning!

Step 1: Wake up

Wake up at the same time every day. I know many of us use an alarm clock to wake up for our workdays, but not on the weekends. Your body is not a big fan of ups and downs. It craves stability. Use your alarm and wake up the same time every day. Once your body gets used to this, you'll thank me.

Would this require you going to bed at the same time every day? Yes, I recommend doing that to get an adequate amount of restful sleep every day. I know that life doesn't always let us get a full night's sleep. You have guests from out of town, so you'll stay up late. Or you have tickets to that sold out concert or sporting event. By no means am I suggesting that you miss out on those things. On the contrary, I'd suggest you take time off of work to do them. (Please don't have your boss email me on that one.) I know that I'm a better employee when I'm rested. My ability to focus improves when I've had a decent amount of sleep. Plus, it's healthy to invest time in things that bring you happiness and pleasure. You're not a robot. When you are happy and rested, you're a better employee, a better family member, a better lover, and a better person for your community.

Step 2: Work Out

There are countless studies on the benefits of exercise. There are countless health-related devices and apps for our phones. There's never been an easier time to track your activity than today! My phone counts my steps, so I do my best to hit ten thousand steps per day. Some days are easier than others. I easily surpassed ten thousand steps when I attended a week's worth of conferences. From walking to the train station to walking around the various conference halls and exhibits, I easily went beyond my goal just by walking around. Be sure to seek approval from your medical provider to make sure what exercises are right for you. I suggest investing the money into a personal trainer, even if it's only for an intro session. You'll learn how to properly use the equipment, and the steps necessary to exercise properly.

If you exercise regularly, you'll have more energy, your stress levels will drop, and your stress management will improve. My suggestion is to work out first thing in the morning. I know many of you don't like waking up early, but if you get up at the same time every day, you can do this as well. Be sure to drink water when you first wake up. It kick-starts your body so you can attack your day.

Step 3: Journal

I love to write. Whether it's a 140-character tweet or a longer blog posts, it helps me to write what I'm thinking. Writing down what's going on your life is good for the soul, as you can empty the things you're thinking onto paper (or a tool like evernote. com). You don't have to write a novel (unless you want to)! I tend to write about my experiences from the day before, or things that come to mind. There are no rules here; it's your journal!

I do recommend that you stick with one app, if you're using technology. Our digital toolboxes can get as cluttered as a junk drawer if you're not careful in what you do. I like Evernote because I have the app on my phone, as well as on my home laptop. It synchronizes the information across all of your devices, so you can pick up where you left off, no matter where you are.

Step 4: Eat Well

I ate a lot of cereal as a kid—the sugary, toy-in-the-bottom-of-the-box kind of cereal. (Not exactly the best way to start your day.) We ask our bodies to put up with a lot during the day, so shouldn't we provide our bodies something to help them fight the good fight? Each person has his or her dietary requirements, so I won't say what you should or shouldn't eat. I'll leave that to you and your nutritional counselor. For my breakfast, I'll always drink water, tea, or coffee, and either eat oatmeal, yogurt with granola and fruit, or the classic bacon-n-eggs.

Step 5: Pick your attire

For an easy entrance into your day, I cannot recommend enough that you pick out your clothes the night before. Did you know your brain consumes calories, just like your body does? Why would you waste your precious morning brainpower by wrestling with what to wear?

If you live in a climate where the weather varies dramatically, then look at your weather app the night before to see what the temperatures will be the next day. In the spring and fall where I live, the mornings can be cold, and the afternoons warm, so layers are important.

Another pro tip I have for your attire (which works especially well for men) is to standardize your outfits. Buy the same kind of socks, undershirts, and underwear. Have at least two weeks' supply of each, so you're not constantly doing laundry. I have a preferred brand of undergarments and socks. By having the same type of socks, matching up pairs is a breeze. Who wants to spend their lives trying to match up socks? Not this guy.

For slacks and shirts, you should have some variety, but go with the style and color (*colour* for Canadians) that best fits you. Spend the money on quality clothes, and they will last you a while. Having clothes that fit you well will help you when you get dressed in the morning. Be sure to mix up your shirts, though—you don't want people thinking you only have one! (It worked for Steve Jobs and Mark Zuckerberg, though, so if you want do it anyway, go for it, boss.)

Step 6: Triage your Calendar

When I began my career, I was an accountant. I had to track my time down to fifteen-minute increments (one firm I worked for billed in twelve-minute increments). It's a habit that many would hate, but I still keep track of every day with a calendar on my laptop that syncs across my devices. I look at my calendar frequently (maybe too frequently) to see what I've worked on, and what's next on my plate.

For a successful day, you should look at the next day the night before. This will mentally prepare you (or scare you) for what you have to face the next day. I also suggest looking at a weeklong view of your calendar, to allow you to batch like items together (when possible).

A deeper subject is when to schedule tasks, meetings, and so forth, throughout your day. Most of us in management have some flexibility on our schedules, but even if you are a front-line worker, you can work with your bosses to establish the best times to meet.

I hope that this gathering of tips will help you have more successful starts to your day. They've served me well in my life, and I'll continue to tweak and grow these steps for years to come.

~Michael
BreakfastLeadership.com

ACKNOWLEDGMENTS

There are so many people to thank who were instrumental in the making of this book—not just the people who encouraged me to put this time in my life to paper, but to those who lived through the 369 days with me.

I thank my Mom and Dad for EVERYTHING—for pulling me out of a school the police would not patrol, and having me attend a school where I met my lifelong friend Joe, the other Joe, Keith, Steve & Amy, and countless other friends and co-workers.

I thank my brother Chad. You see things that I don't, and you have been there for me every single second. You also helped contribute to material in this book, in the things that I didn't see, when I was too busy playing with dominoes.

I thank Sarah, Rachel, and Abigail. Papa loves you, and the women you are becoming. I did my best for you, and will continue to for the rest of my days.

I thank Jenn. I'm sorry you had to go through the dominoes, and for the things that transpired afterwards. You continue to do your best for our daughters, and I am forever grateful.

I thank the countless friends from A.C.C. who have helped my family over the years.

I thank the entire medical team at Windsor's Hotel Dieu Grace Hospital. You helped save my life, and created a restful environment throughout my entire stay. Working in healthcare, I know how hard that can be, and I trust I wasn't a burden to your team.

I thank all of my colleagues throughout my career. The work experiences I've gained continue to help me and to help our respective communities. I hope that I made a positive impact on you, too.

I thank all of my employers who gave me the opportunity to serve their organizations.

I thank Kary Oberbrunner and the entire Igniting Souls Tribe team for their encouragement throughout this process. There were countless times when I was hacked, but as the old Japanese proverb says, "Fall down seven times, stand up eight."

Special thanks to my editor Laura Zeitner. You took my muddled American and Canadian English, and made the book into a gem.

To JCNB and everyone at 99Designs, that made my cover absolutely awesome.

To Chris and his team at JetLaunch. You took my words, and made them jump off the pages!

I thank my Social Media posse on Twitter, Facebook, LinkedIn, and Instagram. Each is a different group, but all of you chose to follow me. I don't know why, but I appreciate it.

I thank Michael Hyatt, John C. Maxwell, Jeff Goins, Grant Baldwin, Tony Robbins, the late Bill Bonds, Bill Ebert, Coach John Wooden, and so many others. I've taken your mentorship to heart, and have applied bits and pieces of what makes you thrive in life, and applied those teachings to my life. I hope I wear it well.

I thank Team AWSOME. (Yes, I know it's misspelled). The encouragement kicks in the pants, love, and support from you made this book possible. I'm excited for what this will bring to the team, going forward. Hold on for a wild ride!

I thank the readers of this book. There are millions of books in the world, but you chose to read this one. I trust that you will be better because of my experiences.

CPSIA information can be obtained
at www.ICGtesting.com
Printed in the USA
LVOW03s0252300917

550608LV00011B/97/P